FIVE CHRISTMAS

ARRANGED BY
PETER SCHUBERT

Uns ist geborn ein Kindelein
Stille Nacht
Noël nouvelet
Les anges dans nos campagnes
Coventry Carol

Mixed Chorus a cappella

C. F. PETERS CORPORATION
NEW YORK LONDON FRANKFURT LEIPZIG

These five carol arrangements may be performed singly or in any combination, and in any order.

UNS IST GEBORN EIN KINDELEIN

1. Uns ist geborn ein Kindelein
   von Maria der Jungfrau rein.
   Alleluja.

2. Des Namen heißt Emanuel,
   wie uns verkündigt Gabriel.
   Alleluja.

3. Das ist so viel als mit uns Gott,
   der uns erlöst aus aller Not.
   Alleluja. Amen.

1. To us is born a little child
   from Mary virgin pure and mild.
   Alleluja.

2. His name is called Emanuel,
   as we were told by Gabriel.
   Alleluja.

3. His name doth mean, "our God with us,"
   who from our sins redeemeth us.
   Alleluja. Amen.

STILLE NACHT

1. Stille Nacht! Heilige Nacht!
   Alles schläft, einsam wacht
   nur das traute heilige Paar.
   Holder Knab im lockigen Haar,
   schlafe in himmlischer Ruh!
   Schlafe in himmlischer Ruh!

2. Stille Nacht! Heilige Nacht!
   Gottes Sohn, O wie lacht
   Lieb' aus deinem göttlichen Mund,
   da uns schlägt die rettende Stund,
   Jesus in deiner Geburt,
   Jesus in deiner Geburt.

3. Stille Nacht! Heilige Nacht!
   Hirten einst Kund gemacht
   Durch der Engel Alleluja
   tönt es laut von Ferne und Nah:
   Jesus der Retter ist da!
   Jesus der Retter ist da!

1. Silent night, holy night,
   all is calm, all is bright
   round yon virgin Mother and Child.
   Holy Infant, so tender and mild.
   sleep in heavenly peace,
   sleep in heavenly peace.

2. Silent night, holy night,
   Son of God, love's pure light
   radiant beams from Thy holy face,
   with the dawn of redeeming grace,
   Jesus, Lord, at Thy birth,
   Jesus, Lord, at Thy birth.

3. Silent night, holy night,
   shepherds quake at the sight,
   glories stream from heaven afar,
   heav'nly hosts sing alleluia;
   Christ, the Savior, is born,
   Christ, the Savior, is born!

NOËL NOUVELET

1. Noël nouvelet, Noël chantons ici.
   Dévotes gens crions à Dieu merci.
   Chantons Noël pour le roi nouvelet.
   Noël nouvelet, Noël chantons ici.

2. L'ange disait: pasteurs partez d'ici.
   L'âme en repos et le cœur réjoui.
   En Bethléem trouverez l'agnelet.
   Noël nouvelet, Noël chantons ici.

1. Sing a new Noel, Noel sing we today.
   All faithful folk, the Lord's mercy we pray.
   Sing we Noel to praise the newborn King.
   Sing a new Noel, Noel sing we today.

2. Angels on high said, shepherds, haste away.
   Set your souls at rest and let your hearts be gay.
   To Bethlehem, come see the Lamb and sing:
   Sing a new Noel, Noel sing we today.

LES ANGES DANS NOS CAMPAGNES

1. Les anges dans nos campagnes
    Ont entonné l'hymne des cieux
    Et l'écho de nos montagnes
    Redit ce chant mélodieux.

    Refrain: *Gloria in excelsis Deo.*

2. Bergers, pour qui cette fête?
    Quel est l'objet de tous ces chants?
    Quel vainqueur, quelle conquête
    Mérite ces cris triomphants?

    Refrain: *Gloria in excelsis Deo.*

3. Ils annoncent la naissance
    Du Libérateur d'Israël,
    Et, pleins de reconnaisance,
    Chantent en ce jour solennel.

    Refrain: *Gloria in excelsis Deo.*

1. Angels we have heard on high,
    sweetly singing o'er the plains,
    and the mountains in reply,
    echoing their joyous strains.

    Refrain: *Gloria in excelsis Deo.*

2. Shepherds, why this jubilee?
    Why your joyous songs prolong?
    What the gladsome tidings be
    which inspire your heav'nly song?

    Refrain: *Gloria in excelsis Deo.*

3. They announce the birth of Jesus
    who redeemeth Israel,
    and their hymn of great thanksgiving
    celebrates this solemn day.

    Refrain: *Gloria in excelsis Deo.*

COVENTRY CAROL

Lully lulla, thou little tiny child,
By by lully lullay, thou little tiny child,
By by lully lullay.

O sisters too,
How may we do
For to preserve this day
This poor youngling
For whom we do sing,
By by lully lullay?

Herod the king
In his raging,
Charged he hath this day,
His men of might
In his own sight,
All young children to slay,
By by lully lullay.

That woe is me,
Poor child, for thee!
And ever morn and day,
For thy parting
Neither say nor sing,
By by lully lullay.

Lully lulla thou little tiny child,
By by lully lullay, thou little tiny child,
By by lully lullay.

PETER SCHUBERT is Associate Professor in the Faculty of Music at McGill University, where he teaches music theory. He conducts the Orpheus Singers (winners in the chamber choir category of the 1996 CBC Competition for Amateur Choirs) and VivaVoce, a professional ensemble. In the 1970s and 80s he conducted the Barnard-Columbia Chorus and the New Calliope Singers in New York City. He has released several recordings with these groups, and he has published an edition of French Noëls (Edition Peters 67723) and a textbook, *Modal Counterpoint, Renaissance Style* (Oxford University Press, 1999).

Cover: late 15th century Spanish manuscript courtesy of Bruce J. Taub
Cover concept by Lisa Stokes Chin
Cover design by Thomas E. Pritchett
Photograph by Allan Chin

duration: ca. 2 min.

Merry Christmas, Pop

Uns ist geborn ein Kindelein

English text by Peter Schubert

from Johann Hermann Schein, *Cantional* (Leipzig, 1627)
arranged by Peter Schubert, 1996

*The top line may be performed by a soloist or a full section, and
the lower four parts by a chorus or instruments (sackbuts and
cornetts are recommended).

Edition Peters 67927

duration: ca. 4 min.

for Kurt Phinney and the New Calliope Singers

Stille Nacht

Text by Joseph Mohr (1792–1848);
English text by John Freeman Young (1820–1885)

Franz Xaver Gruber (1787–1863)
arranged by Peter Schubert, 1991

7

Hol - der Knab ____ im lock - ig - en Haar,
Ho - ly In - fant, so ten - der and mild,
tönt es laut ____ von Fer - ne und Nah:
heav'n - ly hosts ____ sing al - le - lu - ia;

Hol - der Knab __ im lock - ig - en Haar, _____
Ho - ly In - fant, so ten - der and mild, _____
tönt ____ es laut ____ von Fer - ne und Nah: _____
heav'n - ly hosts __ sing al - le - lu - ia; _____

Hol - der Knab __ im lock - ig - en Haar,
Ho - ly In - fant, so ten - der and mild,
tönt ____ es laut ____ von Fer - ne und Nah:
heav'n - ly hosts __ sing al - le - lu - ia;

Hol - der Knab im ____ lock - ig - en Haar,
Ho - ly In - fant, so ten - der and mild,
tönt es laut von ____ Fer - ne und Nah:
heav'n - ly hosts sing ____ al - le - lu - ia;

11

13

14

duration: ca. 2½ min.

pour les Chanteurs d'Orphée

Noël nouvelet

Traditional French
English text by Peter Schubert

Traditional French
arranged by Peter Schubert, 1994

"Panpata" should be pronounced: "pãpətə."

*pronounced "Pān."

duration: ca. $3\frac{1}{2}$ min.

for the Barnard-Columbia Chorus

Les anges dans nos campagnes

Traditional French,
English text, vss. 1 and 2, by James Chadwick (1813–1882);
English text for verse 3 by Peter Schubert

Traditional 18th century French,
arranged by Peter Schubert, 1987

22

30

duration: ca. 3½ min.

for Ben

Coventry Carol

15th century English carol
arranged by Peter Schubert, 1997

32

34